The Muir
Woods

by Katherine Talmadge Sallé

Table of Contents

Introduction 2

Chapter 1
The Old Forest 4

Chapter 2
Muir Woods Gets an Owner 8

Chapter 3
Friends of the Forest 12

Chapter 4
Changes 16

Conclusion 20

Glossary 22

Index 23

Comprehension Check 24

Introduction

Long ago, large forests covered Earth. Imagine how green our planet was! Early humans thought the forests would last forever. They were wrong. Many forests have disappeared. People used the wood from the forests to build houses and for fuel. People cut down forests to make space for cities and farms.

The coast redwood tree was a major member of the ancient North American forest. Today, most coast redwood trees are gone. A few forests have survived. One redwood forest has survived. This forest is Muir Woods.

The redwood trees in Muir Woods are some of the oldest living trees on Earth. Most of these trees are between 500 and 800 years old.

1

The Old Forest

Two thousand years ago, redwood forests stretched along the Pacific Coast of North America. Today, only about 4 percent of the redwood forests remain. These trees live along the foggy coasts of Oregon and Northern California. Part of that forest is just north of San Francisco. This is Muir Woods.

Muir Woods is at a **secluded**, or hidden, place. The setting is a deep **canyon**. In this narrow valley, strong winds cannot **buffet** the redwoods.

Visitors say that Muir Woods is like a **cathedral**—a silent, dark church with a very high ceiling. Muir Woods is silent because moss covers the ground and quiets footsteps. It is dark because the trees grow closely together, shutting out most sunlight. The tall redwoods create the "high ceiling." These are the tallest trees in the world. Most redwood trees grow to be about 200 to 275 feet (61 to 84 m) tall.

The redwood trees in Muir Woods are ⟳ between 500 and 800 years old.

The Homes of the Coast Miwok

The homes of the Coast Miwok looked like upside-down ice cream cones. First, the Miwok made a cone-shaped frame with <u>fir</u> branches. Then they covered each frame with redwood boards, which they called "kotcha."

2,000 years ago Native Americans called the Coast Miwok lived near the canyon. The Miwok came to the redwood canyon on a quest for food. They hunted deer and fished for salmon. They gathered redwood bark and branches to build their homes next to a rocky **cove**.

In 1579, British explorer Sir Francis Drake sailed up the coast. He may have stopped in the cove to repair his ship. Papers from his ship show drawings of homes that look like homes of Miwok.

Language DETECTIVE

Clue: <u>Fir</u> is a homograph. The word *fur* sounds like *fir* but they have different spellings and meanings. Can you find another homograph on page 4?

🎧 Sir Francis Drake

Two hundred years later, Spanish explorers arrived in the same cove. They <u>took over</u> the Miwok lands and built their own settlements. In 1838, the Spanish gave land to an American settler, William Richardson. This land included the redwood canyon.

Until then, people had used the canyon to hunt and fish. However, the nearby town of Yerba Buena was getting bigger. The town needed lumber, or wood, for buildings and homes. The canyon was in danger.

---

take over: to control or own

CHAPTER 2
Muir Woods Gets an Owner

In 1847 Yerba Buena was renamed San Francisco. In 1848, people discovered gold near San Francisco. News about the gold spread quickly. By 1849, many miners moved into the region. The population in San Francisco grew from 800 to 25,000 people in two years.

The town grew bigger, so people needed to build more homes. Logging became an important business. Lumber ships sailed north toward redwood canyon. By 1870, loggers had cut down most of the trees near Muir Woods. But the Muir Woods canyon survived. It was dangerous to land ships in the rocky cove. And it was difficult to log in the steep canyon.

Hikers told people about the canyon's beauty, and it became popular with horseback riders and campers by the late 1880s.

◑ This lumber mill used logs that were cut down from the forests near San Francisco.

In 1892, the Bohemian Club, a San Francisco men's club, took a camping trip in Muir Woods. The members went camping each fall and they went to the canyon. The men agreed that they would buy the place if they liked it. Then they would build a campsite.

They built a huge statue of Buddha in the woods before the trip. The night they camped in Muir Woods was cold and damp. The men decided not to buy it. Instead, they bought another redwood grove in a warmer place. So the woods were left alone.

By 1900 logging tools and methods had improved. It became easier for loggers to cut and move the trees in the canyon. People began to worry about the forest. How long would the woods stay the same?

The Buddha of Bohemian Grove

The Bohemian Club built a Buddha with wood and plaster. They left it in the place where they had camped. The damp fog made the statue fall apart slowly. It was gone by the 1920s. The **grove** where the statue stood is called Bohemian Grove.

🎧 William Kent is the man on the left.

A **conservationist** named William Kent worried about the forest. He wanted to preserve, or save, the forest. He was a businessman and wanted to make money, too. Kent thought he might make money by bringing tourists into the forest, but the land cost $45,000. Both he and his wife thought that was too much money. Kent visited the forest again. "The beauty of the place attracted me," he later wrote. Kent decided to buy the forest. "If we lost all the money we have, and saved those trees, it would be <u>worthwhile</u>," he told his wife. In 1905, he bought Muir Woods.

<u>worthwhile</u>: important enough to spend time or money on

CHAPTER 3

Friends of the Forest

Kent bought the forest just in time. One year later there was a terrible earthquake in San Francisco. Much of the city burned to the ground. People needed lumber to rebuild the city. If Kent had not bought the forest, it would have been reduced to nothing.

Kent had other plans. There was a train that took tourists to nearby Mt. Tamalpais. Kent made a deal with the owners of the train line. They decided to build a railroad track into his canyon to bring in tourists. Kent would build an inn where tourists could stay. Both Kent and the owners would make money.

⊙ The new railway line was called "the crookedest railroad in the world." It was a winding path up the mountain and down into Kent's canyon.

---

just in time: before it is too late

Then Kent had a new challenge. The San Francisco earthquake and fires had frightened people. They demanded a new, larger supply of water. A water company designed a plan. They wanted to <u>dam</u> Redwood Creek for a reservoir. The **reservoir** would drown the forest.

Kent searched for ways to save the forest. Then he learned that Congress had passed a new law in 1906, the Antiquities Act. The President could use the law to save lands "of historic or scientific interest." President Theodore Roosevelt decided to help Kent save the redwoods.

<u>dam</u>: to build a wall to hold back water

Theodore Roosevelt, Friend of the American Wilderness

Theodore Roosevelt became president in 1901. As President, he preserved 148 million acres of forest. He also created five national parks and fifty wildlife preserves. He used the Antiquities Act of 1906 to create eighteen national monuments. One of the first monuments was Kent's redwood canyon.

13

On January 9, 1908, Roosevelt declared the redwood canyon a National Monument. Now the forest belonged to Americans, <u>and</u> no one could cut, flood, or buy it.

Roosevelt wanted to name the forest Kent's Woods. But Kent chose the name Muir Woods to honor America's greatest conservationist, John Muir.

🎧 John Muir at Muir Woods

John Muir loved nature. When he was young, Muir had a bad accident and almost went blind. He made himself a promise. If he regained his sight, he would spend his life enjoying the sights of nature. Muir's eyesight returned, so he sailed to San Francisco. He asked a man at the dock for directions. "Where do you want to go?" the man asked.

"Any place that is wild," Muir said.

Clue: The word <u>and</u> is a conjunction and tells you that the sentence is a compound sentence. Can you find another compound sentence on page 9?

Muir went to many wild places. He especially loved the Sierra Mountains and redwood forests. He fought hard to save trees and land. He wrote books to persuade others to save nature. In 1892, he helped to form the Sierra Club, which works to preserve nature.

John Muir was delighted that Kent named the forest after him. Muir wrote this letter to Kent.

February 6, 1908

Dear Mr. Kent:

Seeing my name in the tender and deed of the Tamalpais Sequoias was a surprise of the pleasantest kind. This is the best tree-lover's monument that could possibly be found in all the forests of the world. You have done me great honor and I am proud of it.

Saving these woods from the axe and saw, from money-changer and water changers, and giving them to our country and world is in many ways the most notable service to God and man I've heard of since my forest wanders began. . . .

Ever yours,

John Muir

CHAPTER 4

Changes

William Kent was elected to Congress in 1910. In 1916, he introduced the bill that formed the National Park Service. It had two **missions**. They were to **conserve** wild lands and to make sure people enjoy them.

At first, people enjoyed the wild lands but did little to conserve them. There were few rules in the forest. People **trampled** the moss and ferns. They dug up wildflowers. People even burned campfires. Muir Woods was a mess.

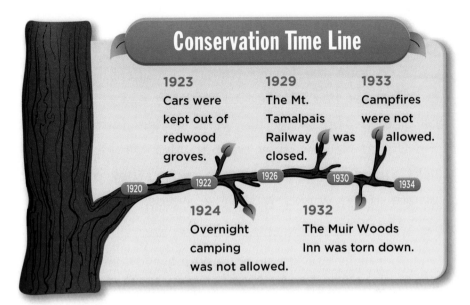

Conservation Time Line

1923
Cars were kept out of redwood groves.

1929
The Mt. Tamalpais Railway was closed.

1933
Campfires were not allowed.

1920 • 1922 • 1926 • 1930 • 1934

1924
Overnight camping was not allowed.

1932
The Muir Woods Inn was torn down.

⌕ In the 1920s and 1930s, steps were taken to reduce damage to Muir Woods.

People made rules to help Muir Woods. But more people began to visit. A new bridge, the Golden Gate Bridge, opened. This meant that it was easier to get to Muir Woods.

Then, in 1942, Muir Woods got a new ranger, Lawson Brainerd. Brainerd removed ten of the fourteen footbridges that crossed Redwood Creek. He also removed the picnic tables. Then he put fences along the trails.

Brainerd's work made Muir Woods a safe place for ancient trees.

↻ Lawson Brainerd fenced the trails to prevent people from walking on the moss and ferns.

In May 1945, many world leaders came to San Francisco. World War II had ended, and the leaders came to form the United Nations. President Franklin D. Roosevelt had planned to lead the event. Sadly, he died in April. After the world leaders formed the United Nations, they went to Muir Woods. They held a ceremony in a redwood grove. They placed a plaque in the woods with these words.

> Here in this grove of enduring redwoods, preserved for **posterity**, members of the United Nations Conference on International Organization met on May 19, 1945 to honor the memory of Franklin Delano Roosevelt, thirty-first president of the United States, chief architect of the United Nations and apostle of peace for all mankind.

Other plaques have been dedicated in Muir Woods. William Kent had a favorite tree. It was a Douglas fir. Kent died in 1928, but the William Kent Tree is still alive and almost 400 years old. In 1976, one tree became the Bicentennial Tree. The park rangers chose a tree that was 200 years old. That tree honors our nation's two-hundredth birthday.

---

dedicate: to set something apart from others to honor someone

Conclusion

By 1900, many redwood forests were gone. Some trees were cut for lumber. Other trees were cut to build new towns and farms, but Muir Woods survived. Its location saved it from loggers. Later, people helped to save it.

Muir Woods is beautiful today. However, it is still a "recovering forest." The National Park Service is trying to help it become the forest it was long ago.

Muir Woods is once again the **habitat** of woodland animals. The brown bears and grizzlies are gone, but bobcats, deer, and fox have returned. The salmon and trout have returned. Ladybugs migrate to Muir Woods each summer. They return to the same spots every year.

Muir Woods is open every day. Visit and look up as high as you can. You will never be able to see all the way to the tops of those ancient redwood trees. The trees are survivors. They will remain.

⬆ Owls have returned to Muir Woods.

Glossary

buffet to blow about very strongly when hit by strong winds (page 5)

canyon a long, narrow valley between high cliffs, often with a stream flowing through it (page 4)

cathedral a large and important church (page 5)

conserve to save and protect natural resources such as water, land, and trees from harm or waste (page 16)

conservationist a person who works to conserve natural resources (page 11)

cove a small sheltered bay or inlet (page 6)

grove a group of trees standing together (page 10)

habitat the area where a plant or animal naturally grows or lives (page 21)

mission a job or promise complete a goal (page 16)

posterity future generations (page 18)

reservoir a natural or man-made lake in which water is stored for people to use (page 13)

secluded shut off or kept apart from others; hidden or alone (page 4)

trample crushed or destroyed by the people or animals running over something (page 16)

Index

Antiquities Act, *13*

Bicentennial Tree, *19*

Bohemian Club, *10*

Brainerd, Lawson, *17*

Coast Miwok, *6–7*

Drake, Sir Francis, *7*

Gold Rush, *8*

Golden Gate Bridge, *17*

Kent, William, *11–15, 16, 19*

lumber industry, *7, 8–9, 11, 12*

Mount Tamalpais, *12, 16, 17*

Muir, John, *14–15*

National Park Service, *16, 21*

Richardson, William, *7*

Roosevelt, Franklin D., *18*

Roosevelt, Theodore, *13–14*

San Francisco, *4, 8, 9, 10, 12, 13, 14, 18*

United Nations, *18*

Yerba Buena (see *San Francisco*)

Comprehension Check

Summarize

Complete the Main Idea Chart with the class. Summarize the story. You can use the chart to help you organize your ideas.

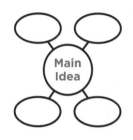

Think and Compare

1. Read the last paragraph on page 4. Tell how a cathedral and Muir Woods are alike and different. *(Compare and Contrast)*

2. What can you do to protect nature so it stays clean and healthy? *(Apply)*

3. Which person do you think helped the Muir Woods the most? Explain your answer. *(Evaluate)*